The Naked Soul of a Bearded Man

Michael B. North

Acknowledgments

Cover photo credit goes to
Natalie J. Devore of
DeVoreVision!
Email:
summerchild718@
gmail.com
Website:
www.DevoreVision.com
You truly are an amazing
photographer and an amazing
friend.

I look forward to working with
you again in the near future.

Thank you to Kenny Santos for
taking the time to re-edit the
book.

Special Thanks to Emanuel
D'Argenio for designing the
cover for me. We lost touch for
many years my friend. Let's

never do that again. You truly
are family to me.
For any inquiries, please
contact him @
GsGraphicsStudio@gmail.com

To my closest friends, Abby,
Ruzma, & Magdeleyne,;
Thank you for your support.
You ladies helped me believe in
myself when I was at my worst.
I am forever grateful to each of
you, and the love that you have
provided to me.

To my brother Eric, You have
always believed in my vision,
even before I realized I had
one. It's a pleasure being your
twin. I am very proud of the
man and father you have
become. The best is yet to come
for the both of us…

To the most important being of all,
For there is only "ONE"

Thank you for pushing me to my breaking point, and kindly reeling me back, into the warmth of your embrace…

To my daughter
Arianna,

You are my saving
grace, and by far, my
greatest gift from
God.
This book is
dedicated to you my
child…

Contents

Chapter One:

"Be aware of those that are out to
break your heart. Be more aware
of those are out to break your
spirit." (M.B.North)

Chapter Two:

"It's true that our children are like
sponges, and absorb whatever we
put into them. Put in hate, and
you'll create a monster. Put in love,
and you'll create something better
than yourself. "   (M.B.North)

Chapter Three:

"It's not that I'm special. I just feel things differently. " (M.B.North)

Chapter Four:

(Blog) "Five more Minutes"
(By M.B. North)

Chapter Five:

"Be the Man that doesn't walk out of her life. Be the man that her father wasn't." (M.B.North)

Chapter Six:

"If you are a father to a little girl, and you are looking for love, then date the kind of woman you want your daughter to grow to be."
(M.B.North)

Chapter Seven:

"Find your peace. Avoid the war in others." (M.B.North)

Chapter Eight:

(Blog) "Have you Ever?"
(By M.B. North)

Chapter Nine:

"When I wasn't happy, I smiled anyway. I would stand in front of a mirror, and I would practice smiling. Even though I did not like what I saw in the mirror then, I would do it regardless. Until eventually, my smiling came naturally, and so did my happiness." (M.B. North)

Chapter Ten:

"My father died with a picture of my mother in his hand. That is the definition of being loved by a man." (M.B.North)

Chapter Eleven:

Chapter Twelve:

"I want to be everything that you have ever dreamt about. I want to be everything every other man failed to be. I want to help fill up the hole that he left inside of you, and I want to change the world with you by my side. But most importantly, when it's finally time to give me your hand, I want to be the man that replaces your father."
(M.B.North)

Chapter Thirteen:

"Why do so many men run towards a war, but away from love? Perhaps the more important battle that you need to face, is not in another country, but in fact inside of you." (M.B.North)

Chapter Fourteen:

"I want to build something that will be here, when I no longer am." (M.B. North)

Chapter Fifteen:

"There are two reasons why we suffer. The first is to teach us a lesson. The second is so that our children won't have to." (M.B.North)

I wonder if every author, while writing their first book, asked themselves the same question that I am asking myself right now, "Is this how I should start my book?"

So after hours of deliberation, this was the final outcome.

So many people come to me these days, asking me for the solution to their problems, but there is something I have not told any of them. Perhaps now would be the best time, in the very beginning of my first book?

I want to first state that I do not have all the answers, and at this point in my life, there is the distinct possibility that I may have more questions than answers. It also seems that I may have inherited more problems too. I guess that comes with the territory, and it certainly reminds me of what my parents would say to me often as a little boy, "You should be careful what you wish for."

This statement applies towards too many things in my life right now, and if I think too much about it, I give myself a headache. Ok, now I am just beginning to ramble. Anyway, Welcome everyone to my first book.

My name is Michael North, and here a few words, courtesy of my soul...

CHAPTER ONE

"Be aware of those that are out to break your heart. Be more aware of those that are out to break your spirit…"

This particular **quote** takes me to a very significant time in my life. Back to when I thought I had most of the answers, and finally possessing the ability to say that I loved myself. Thirty-one years is a long time to wait, and it is difficult to remember how to smile, when I do not have

many memories of myself as a child, truly being that happy.
Damn, I don't think I've ever been that honest with anyone, and that would include myself.

Some people let themselves become quite bitter because of their painful life experiences. I do understand why, I just do not have to agree with it. Everyone knows that monsters create monsters, but they are not what we necessarily see on the big screen though. Some may live down the block, some may live next door to you, some may live in your home, and others you may run into, as you grow and move through life. Each and every one of those monsters will leave a permanent mark on your soul, and the outcome of your life and your human and spiritual development, will also be very much influenced by them. For many, it is often difficult to see the blessings from these so-called teachers, when the only thing they remind you of is pain and suffering.

I began to realize at an early age, that I loved very differently when it came to personal relationships. I can also freely state that, although I rarely fall in love, I do fall very hard.

I am now able to prepare myself for any disappointment. It does not mean that it hurts any less; it just means that I realize that it will not kill me. For the end of any significant relationship will determine just that — the end of that relationship, not the end of my happiness.

I once loved a woman with everything that I was, and that also included my soul. You see that is where I made my mistake. In retrospect, I can laugh it at now, but I can assure you, I certainly was not laughing back then. How could I have been so blind? How could I have been so foolish? The soul is only borrowed by human beings, but we can have our souls touched by love, or by giving love to other beings, human and non-human alike. A connection so to speak. But the soul does not belong to us; it can only belong to the universe, which means it belongs to God.

Now back to this woman…

I loved the way that she smelled. I loved the way that she smiled. I loved the shape of her eyes, her touch, and her ability to look right into me. That kind of look could bring any man to his knees. She certainly brought me to mine – just as my mother must have brought my father to his knees. She was just the karma I was looking for — I had been at peace and made good with my bad karma for quite some time before meeting her, so there was no possible way that this woman would choose to ever scar me. Or so I presumed.

There is also the fact, that there would be no story to tell, if our love story did not turn and take another direction, south in particular. It did not take very long before this woman began to speak to me in a less than respectful manner. It also did not take very long before she began raising her hand to me as well.

You see, my father was a strong man, and wise man; he told me that for the right one, the right woman that is, it would sometimes become very difficult, but it did not mean that she was not worth loving. I knew that that this woman had deep rooted problems long before she became mine, I just wanted to be the one to stick around and fix them for her, just as my father and I were discussing all those years ago.

All I had ever done was run away from every relationship that I was in, and for the first time in my life, I got tired of running. I just wanted to stay.

Have you ever loved someone so much that it consumed you? When the most important thing for you is just to see your partner happy, the way that you are, but what you realize is that nothing you do ever seems like it is enough. Well this is true, and because you will be too busy trying your hardest to plug your partner's lifelong holes, you will eventually become weak, and in the process you will lose yourself, and fall into a beautiful dark abyss.

The next year was torturous. Extreme highs and lows were the forecast inside of my home. I felt as if I was lost in the middle of a storm daily, and I never knew where to find salvage. But eventually I did find salvage, in addition to finding my salvation. Now I had the ability to find peace anywhere, even in the middle of my very own war.

I do recall telling that woman, midway through the relationship, that I would eventually leave her, if she did not address me with the love, kindness, and the respect that I provided to her. She never took me very seriously, and I am the kind of man that likes to make good on my promises. Plus my sanity and patience were reaching a new high or low, (depending how you look at it) and at that point, I believed I had found exactly what I was looking for.
I want to be honest with all of you.

I knew the relationship was going to fail from the very beginning. From the moment I saw her I knew she that would change my life forever, and show me something that no other partner had ever taught me. A teacher so to speak, who would teach me a very dark art form. Although I knew I would never use it, I simply needed to experience it to understand how to face it, if it were to ever come my way again. I call these experiences, trial and error tests for the soul. I believe they are necessary to teach us what real strength is. The process also brings you closer to God, so the pain is always worth it.

I do recall allowing my soul to get stepped on and still deciding to stay. This was not pity or stupidity. This was my heart telling me to be the one man she would be able to depend on; the man that would love her properly, and treat her better than she treated herself. I knew the consequences if I failed. So I went into battle with nothing but my heart on my sleeve, and a hope that I could be the one to make it better.

I lost that battle with honor, and as graciously as possible, I bowed my way out, and made way off into the sunset without her. Poetic?

Absolutely not! But it was another battle that left me with new scars, & the one lesson I couldn't see for myself until I walked away and began to write again. Humility. For you see you could never find God, without first experiencing humility. That particular heartbreak tore a hole in my soul, and the only thing I had left to do was to fill it with the love of God, & for this, I thank you my dear…

CHAPTER TWO

"It's true when they say that our children are like sponges and absorb whatever we put into them. Put in hate and you'll create a monster. Put in love and create something better than yourself."

It was said a million times yesterday, and will be said an additional million today. Our children are the future. So if that truly is the case, and if we have any kind of compassion within us, shouldn't we all want our children to be better than us? Think about a child. Think about what kind of person he or she may become. Then realize and understand that it all starts with you. Our children are like sponges. Tell them to commit crimes for money, and you may create the best bank robber of all time, but tell that child to love God, and to spread the message of God, and watch how he or she will heal others.

A perfect and personal example of this was my life prior to finding God. I used to be one of the worlds monsters. The lack of affection and love from a very prominent female in my life, caused me to have self-conflicted issues from the moment I was born. I do not recall being told back then that I was loved by her, and if I was, it was said very few and far between. It was shown even less. I wanted the approval of her for so long, yet all I was ever told, was that I would amount to nothing. I longed for her embrace, but only received it from my father.

As I grew older, I would look at the

mirror often, and remember being disgusted with what I saw there. I hated my nose, and my eyes always looked so sad. Perhaps it was because they were only a reflection of what I felt inside at the time. Let me not forget to mention my weight and my obsession with it. How dreadful it was for me to be thin. Especially when I compared myself to my father, who was a full statured man. He stood 6ft 3in and over 220 pounds. I on the other hand was 6ft 1in, and barely 150 pounds. Lanky and scrawny best described me at the time.

My father knew of the issues that I had, and knew the root of them as well, but would never address them. He would simply state, "I was a thin boy like you, and you'll appreciate it when you get older." My low self-esteem carried on into my teens.

Convincing the opposite sex to be attracted to me was not a problem; the actual problem lied within the way that I still continued to view myself. By the time I reached nineteen years of age, I realized how weak I had become, and found myself often hurt at the hands of women. I had become furious with the idea that as a man, I could so easily submit to a woman. I vowed after that heartbreak, to never be the victim again.

That day a monster was born.

By the time I was twenty-one I had become a savage, and I realized that I could no longer be controlled by any woman. This pleased me immensely. For I was now the aggressor, which provided me with full control at all times. Nothing was sweeter than the taste of revenge, and for the next ten years of my life, I would make every woman pay for the actions of one.

It seemed that throughout my entire life, heartache and loss were the only ways I was able to find myself. That was certainly the case once my father passed away. His death finally brought us closer together, and there is a part of me that believes that he knew that his death would do just that. The truth is, I could easily have decided to turn my back on my mother, but that isn't what God would have wanted. My mother was simply repeating the same behavior pattern that she learned from her mother. She also learned to forgive her mother for her shortcomings. So why couldn't I?

The truth is, forgiveness will set you free, and choosing love always brings you closer to God. I can say that I did not get the mother that I wanted growing up, but I can also say that God gave me the mother that I needed now. Our relationship today is now mended, and I thank my father and our Creator for that. I love you mom.

CHAPTER THREE

"It's not that I am special. I just feel things differently."

Actually, I feel things inside of my soul. It just so happens that it is the same place I also choose to speak from. Many people ask why I am like this, and why am I so different? It is not complicated. I am simply a product of my life experiences, just as anyone else is, but I have chosen to go deep within myself for the answers that most seek in the outside world, while also not letting my painful experiences revert me into a monster.

Which takes me back to an earlier part of my life. My childhood to be exact. I recall at times being overly sensitive to the point that I could make myself sick. I didn't know how to control it then. All I knew was that I could feel pain in a way that felt different, more personal and less desirable. From an early age, I was told too many times from so-called important peers, that I would be a failure. I think a part of me began to believe that, and as a result the smallest disrespect to my heart, always seemed to injure me internally. What made this worse, was that I lived with this secret for all of my childhood, and never told a soul of what it did to me. Granted, I did cry, but what child didn't cry when their feelings were hurt? The adults just chalked it up to oversensitivity.

Relationships with women are a part of growing up, so as expected, I did partake in the festivities of dating. I recall being around fifteen years old the first time I experienced heartbreak from a woman. Yes it was puppy love, but you couldn't tell that to my heart. It was the first time that I had ever met someone that I found so attractive, so beautiful, and so compelling. My older brother and her older cousin attended the same university, which was how the plans came about, and when we finally met, the connection was instantaneous.

I was only fifteen, but my heart wanted what it wanted. We would spend hours on the phone, and I would at times leave my center of education, to go to the Bronx, from Westchester-County, just to pick her up from school. We were both sophomores and singing the praises of love each and every time we connected. Spring was in the air, even through the harshness of a New York winter. I couldn't get enough of her, and her petite size, made her absolutely adorable.

I stood 6ft 1in, while she was a mere, 4ft 9in. The height difference was quite noticeable, but something that foolish couldn't hinder our love. Eventually her birthday was to come, April 1st was the day, and I remember needing to somehow find a way to give her a gift that no other before me could have. I was sixteen now, an older man, but without a job. This meant that I couldn't afford to buy her a thing, forcing me to be somewhat creative.

Her family decided to throw her a birthday party in their apartment, and I wasn't going to miss it. I remember arriving and seeing her best friends there, who I was already acquainted with. We greeted one another by kissing on the cheek and hugging with love. Dinner was eventually served and everyone was now mingling. Each of them were telling stories of what was happening in their lives, and discussing the local drama and rumors, that only live on the tongues of gossiping serpents. I simply nodded my head, pretending that I cared, and only thinking about wanting to hold the hand of my girlfriend. Then my moment came. It was time to celebrate her sixteenth birthday. I recall it being dark, and the only light that could be seen in that room, came from the candles on top of her birthday cake. She cut the first piece, and I knew I had to do something to get the attention of her, and everyone else in that room, before the lights were turned back on.

Here was my moment, and as my heart raced, I somehow managed to gather up enough courage to ask everyone in the room to please lower their voices. I walked closer towards the candle light and reached into my pocket, and pulled out a poem that I had written for her. I then looked at her and began to read my words of affection. I poured out my heart that evening, and when the poem came to an end, the room stood in complete silence. I then looked up at the young woman that I loved, and I realized at that moment, that perhaps it was possible, that she may have loved me, just as much as I loved her. She tried to muster up a "thank you" and an "I love you" but the tears of joy and her sobs kept drowning out everything she could have possibly uttered out. I just walked closer to her and wrapped my arms around her and said, "thank you for loving me." I knew then I loved differently.

Prior to that, I thought only pain drove me, but here, at the tender age of sixteen, I realized love was felt more deeply than anything I could have possibly imagined, and it was the first time I felt close to God. But it wasn't to last. Eventually her parents feared of our relationship becoming too intense, and openly admitting that they didn't want their child to end up pregnant. We weren't having sex, but they refused to listen, and shortly thereafter, the relationship was officially over. I remember how it felt when I realized I would never be able to call her mine again. The place that knew God, now had a hole that was being filled with more pain. Suddenly I felt like that small child again. Alone in the world, with the belief that no one loved me, and anyone that ever did, would never stay.

Many years soon passed, and eventually I was to find my spirituality and a deeper connection with God. It was going to be a bit more interesting to now experience what came attached to feeling things differently.

I recall being in New York City one odd winter day, with a relative of mine. She and I decided, that since the weather was going to be unusually warm, that we should spend it together walking around one of the greatest cities in the world. So off we went to walk from the upper west side of Manhattan, to downtown east Canal Street. I recall mentioning to myself, perfect weather with perfect company. We eventually found ourselves in Chinatown, by a small park, which had a fence that housed at least 20 people behind it that day. Also behind it stood an older man, at least 60 years old, and a woman who was about half his age, who I imagined to be his daughter. I marveled at the way that they interacted with one another. For there was love between them, which meant God was present in both of their lives. I now felt a bit more connected to them. But there was something that was concerning me. It was the health of the older gentleman who appeared to be quite ill. Besides being attached to a breathing apparatus, he also moved very slowly. It only took a few short minutes to realize that my world was going to be greatly affected by these people. By these strangers…

I was still standing by the fence when it happened. It began when I wished this man wellness. I did not need to know of this man's life to wish him good health, energy, and love. Perhaps today, I should share with him some of mine?

At that moment I lost control of myself. I suddenly began to feel weak. My legs trembled, my stomach hurt, and I was losing focus. I had to think fast. I quickly grabbed onto the fence and held on as hard as I could without collapsing. It lasted for 10-15 seconds I believe, but felt like minutes. The pain was excruciating and my heart was broken. I suddenly felt that I needed to cry, but instead I decided to smile. For although I did feel that man's pain inside of me, I realized there

was the possibility that he too felt
my good wishes towards him. I also
believe in my heart, that I truly
helped him, and that he lived just a
bit longer, because someone asked
God for that favor.

I walked away with an experience
that is still worth talking about today.
I realized that God is present at all
times, and we all need to connect
with our spiritual selves and wish
more people more love. I realized at
that moment, that once again in my
life, I did in fact feel things
differently.

CHAPTER FOUR

5 More Minutes

Five more minutes. I'm not even
sure what for. Maybe to make love to
you just a bit longer? Five more
minutes to perhaps enjoy this feeling.
The feeling I get, each and every
time I have the desire to just write.
Five more minutes to wonder about
what it is that has just happened to
me. How I became like this, and how
I began to believe in something more
then just the small world I lived in
before today? Or do I need an
additional 5 minutes to think about
my daughter? How much I believe in

her, and how much she represents everything I will fail to become. Five more minutes to sleep in this bed, wishing I had never set the alarm in the first place. Five more minutes to hold you in my arms, before we experience reality and realize, we have to leave each other's side once again.

Five more minutes to think about my mother. To think about how much she's helped, hurt, and assisted in molding me into the man I am today. Five more minutes to read this book. To read this piece of fiction, and figure out every way possible to make it my reality. Five more minutes to stay on the phone with you. I don't care that you're at work. I admit freely that I have childish behavioral issues, and I just don't want you to hang up. Five more minutes to look up at the sky. To play with the clouds, and imagine me flying and looking down at all of God's creations. Five more minutes to stay on vacation. I know that it will soon end, but I need to enjoy the moment for as long as I possibly can with you.

Five more minutes to spend time missing my father. Telling him how much I still need him, love him, and assuring him there isn't another that could ever take his place. Or perhaps I just need an additional five minutes to breathe and sigh? Realizing five minutes wouldn't have changed a thing. Because even if I had gotten to you five minutes sooner, you still would have died.

I think I need five minutes to cry…

CHAPTER FIVE

"Be the man who doesn't walk out of her life. Be the man her father wasn't."

This statement says so much in so few words. There is a harsh truth behind it, and many that will read this, or hear of this, may sadly be able to relate to it as well.

Picture a little girl. A beautiful creation of God. Her first breath, her first sight, her first tears, and her first smell of this earth. Miracles are already beginning to unfold. Through these beautiful brief moments, and as time continues to pass, she will gain the ability to see and understand more. She will learn to walk, she will learn to talk, and she will now begin to express herself as a little person. No longer an innocently naive infant, her instincts have come into play, and she will now be exploring more of the world. This will happen sooner than you can prepare for, and she will need love from the day she is born, from everyone and anyone that will come into contact with her. Including those who we commonly refer to as strangers.

Now imagine the possibilities that can unfold knowing that she has love from everyone around her. Imagine what she can grow into. The beauty alone sends chills down my spine, and tears of joy to my heart. The love provided to her early on, will give her much more strength, patience, and peace, as she grows older. She now has more of a chance to face and to endure the hardships that unfortunately come attached to this world. For true beauty and happiness, only come to those who understand what it is to suffer. Our roles as parents are to make sure our children suffer less than we did, until the day comes, where not one soul in this world will know the definition of pain. Until then, we can simply hope and pray.

Now imagine a slightly different chain of events. Imagine a little girl without a father. Who will show her what a good man is, and how will she know whom to love, once she grows older and is interested in the opposite sex? I have come across far too many women throughout my life, which sadly fell into this category. Life early on can already be a struggle for so many, even when they have the key components to happiness. So imagine how the game may be played, when you take away one of its most valued players?

In comparison to a war, that would be like fighting the battle with only one arm. Leaving no possibility of protecting yourself. That isn't exactly fair, now is it? Now the possibility of her making poor decisions in life has increased dramatically. Especially when it comes to her dating partners. I have seen women date the same kind of man more than once, and later wonder how they ended up in the position they always found themselves in. One example is the woman who dates the kind of man who abuses her. She seems to think that she loves him much more than anyone else, and cannot seem to figure out why she will not let him go. Even after he tells her that she is worthless, and that no one else would want her, she will find herself begging for more of his attention.

The poor child never learned her self worth, and does not realize that it can never be found in a man. Or what about the woman who becomes the monster? She was faced with some of the most difficult hardships that could have easily ended up with her taking her own life, but she instead becomes the aggressor. Now everything that she hated in men, will become her strongest attributes. She will then run around in the world, breaking the hearts of any man that comes across her path. Her anger and resentment towards the male species has now made her a dangerous weapon, and she carelessly waves that same weapon around, not caring who is cut by her tongue or hands.

I pray that more fathers take an active role and responsibility in their daughters' lives. This isn't about being the #1 dad in the world, but it is about being the #1 father to your children…

CHAPTER SIX

"If you are a father to a little girl and you're looking for love, then date the kind of woman you want your daughter to grown into."

I want to mention that I am a very lucky man. I want to also mention that I do in fact have a wonderful young daughter, who is a major highlight of my life. I will go as far as saying that she easily becomes a highlight in anyone's life, who is lucky enough to come into contact with her. A constant reminder that I have in fact done something right with my life.

By the grace of God, her mother and I have become, and have remained good friends over the years, and together we have raised a blessing of a child, while living separate lives in separate homes. The betterment of our child was what was always most important. We realized that this was the only way to bring happiness to each other as well. Speaking from experience, let me first mention that this is all just my opinion, but I do hope you can see the sincerity and kindness in my advice, so that every single father can raise a wonderful child, and in the process possibly meet the woman he is supposed to spend the rest of his life with. I had pent up anger and disappointment in the failing of my relationship with her mother at that time, and didn't want to take it out on anyone.

I must admit, I met some amazing women after my daughter was born. Some that would have been a great mother figure to my dearest Arianna. However, my negativity and anger would ruin every relationship that I had, right up until the day that my father passed away. But I feel it should not take a tragedy to change the direction of your life. That just does not seem right to me, but of course it was necessary for me to find myself.

I also began to realize that my daughter was getting older. I began to think to myself, what kind of female role model would she look up to, if I never kept any of them around for longer than 20 minutes? I personally have made my share of mistakes with women, and I can also say that I was not careful enough with who I brought around my child. Granted, each of them were kind and loving to her, but none of them are here today. I take full responsibility for that, and yes it does hurt me, that for one reason or another, anyone she may have become attached to, are no longer a part of her life. This is the reason that the only women who should meet your child, should be your friends and family only. For when the situation doesn't work out, multiple parties always wind up getting hurt, and in every case, the most important person that loses is your child.

The first thing you need to think about is whom you will be bringing around your child. Many of you may have had a great relationship and upbringing with your mothers. Consider yourselves blessed. If your mother was as wonderful as you claim her to be, then perhaps it would make sense to date someone who possesses her same redeeming qualities. I happen to agree with the following statement, "Let the woman you marry, take the position your mother once held."

The truth is, men are simply over-grown children when it comes to their emotions. We all love to be spoiled by the women who loves us. I am not saying that a woman should spoil her man rotten, but she should spoil him with love. She should also know the difference between simply stroking a man's ego, and actually showing him the love he deserves. His child loves him unconditionally. His mother loves him unconditionally. Shouldn't the woman who he wants to be with do the same?

It gets a little trickier when it comes to men who do not have a good female role model in their lives. A dysfunctional relationship with ones' mother often creates a dysfunctional presence in many, or if not in all of the relationships that a man will have with the women he dates throughout his life. Unless he is able to one day recognize that the cycle must end with him. One can only pray that is the case.

I have already mentioned what is important in regards to similarities, but what about her traits or behavior that should be important to you? One thing every parent or non-parent should have is patience. The woman that you want to be with will need to have the patience to deal with children. That will always make or break the relationship. Her patience and understanding will also come into play when it comes to making time for your child. If she cannot understand that you need time to spend with your own child, then why would you waste another second speaking to her? Personality is very important. Pay attention to how she behaves. Especially with her treatment to others; if she is kind to those who don't directly benefit her, then there is a strong possibility that she is worth having in your life, and in the life of your daughter. In addition, she should also be a role model for your child. Your daughter should have a strong and loving woman in her life, to discuss some of the things you will not be able to on your own, as she grows older. Lastly, make sure that that the woman you once again choose, is both loving and affectionate. This will not only benefit your pride and joy, but it will also benefit you, when you need the love of a good woman.

CHAPTER SEVEN

"Find your peace. Avoid the war in others."

Some of us choose live in a dysfunctional state, while others do not have much of a choice and are merely born into it. What we never seem to realize is that we have a choice to not end up, or turn into the "things" or people, that we dislike the most. For many, it is hard to see hope, when the people or places we may live in, or are surrounded by, offer us nothing but negative energy.

It is been studied and proven for

many years now, that children carry the genetic make-up of both of their parents. This includes characteristics that can make us just as great, or better than our parents could ever be, but it can also mean, that we can take on, or later develop diseases that our parents blood lines may have embedded. I believe the case is just same, when it comes to spirituality or lack thereof; parents can pass on their gifts or curses to their children. I do not need science or doctors to prove this. I am living proof that my spirituality was a gift to me. The day my father planted his seed into the womb of my mother, that deal was sealed. My late father was very spiritual, and my mother has particular "gifts" that she kindly passed onto me as well. Unfortunately, I also received their demons. Luckily I have learned how to keep them at bay, or how to defeat them entirely. But what about the people that do not have the spiritual or mental awareness to heal themselves?

I ask you to imagine something; what if your mother or father suffered from some sort of mental illness? Now also try to imagine that same parent being abusive. Picture a child who is but ten or eleven years old, who is already experiencing uneasiness or anxiety. Would you be able to blame them for what they are feeling? It won't be long now before he or she may develop that same mental illness that their parent had, due to the constant trigger or triggers within that home. How is he or she ever going to know what peace is, when war is all they have ever experienced? The war in their minds, the war their bodies, and the war that's now in the real world.

Will you expect that person to know how to treat other people? Especially when they do not know how to treat themselves. This person only knows pain. So the easiest thing to do would be to inflict that pain upon oneself, and eventually towards anyone who wants to help them. It is hard to accept kindness or love in world that only understand chaos.

I can speak freely about such a subject matter. My unhappiness years ago caused me to hurt everyone that had my best interests in mind. I trusted no one, no matter how sincere their tears were. They all came to know my pain & I refused to let anyone get close to me. I lied, I cheated, and I broke the will of far too many women. For when I was not destroying lives and taking away love from other people; I was selling drugs or committing random acts of violence towards perceived enemies.

The story of my life is not uncommon, so why would it be a surprise to anyone else, when another broken being fulfills such a sad prophecy? Our social environments are nurturing more monsters. When will we finally see that the worlds' problems first begin in our own homes? It certainly began in mine!

I suppose therapy would be a good way to heal this kind of person, but does it always have to be from a doctor? While I do believe that they do a great job for many people, I also believe that there is something just as therapeutic and much more nourishing to the soul. Love. For everyone knows that love can heal and warm the coldest of hearts. It healed mine, so why would I not believe that it could heal others?

Unfortunately there are those that become so wrapped up in their own mental wars that they choose purposely to hurt others and have no interest in finding their way back to humanity. Hurting others has now become the norm to them, and a sick sadistic game that can only be enjoyed at the expense of another person's feelings. I have met many like this. They find it amusing to be hurt and to hurt others. Whether it be through cheating in a relationship, or committing acts of violence against people they perceive to be there enemies.

My belief? They will be saved one day, but only through prayer. It's sometimes better to keep your distance from these people, but not your love. For to give them a prayer with love, is to give them the blessings of God, and that is exactly what God would expect of us…

CHAPTER EIGHT

"Have You Ever?"

Have you ever looked out at the sky and wondered if there was more to our existence? Or perhaps you are one of those that only sees and believes in what is precisely ten feet in front of them? Have you ever had the opportunity to tell a woman that you truly love her and really meant it? Not just through song and word, but through something deeper.

Something that cannot be seen with the human eye, but still felt on and under your partner's skin. Have you ever helped someone in need? A stranger perhaps? Not just through generous offerings of financial bearing, but taking the time to sit down and asking how he or she was feeling on that particular day? Have you ever jumped into your automobile and taken a ride to nowhere? With no destination in mind, because you simply aren't looking for one. Where you just inhale life and every single one of its magnificent sights in motion. Have you ever gone to the beach to feel what the sand is like? Planting your feet firmly within the ground and just letting go? Closing your eyes and tapping into that deeper energy source that most either aren't aware of, or refuse to believe in its' existence… it does exist.

Have you ever just taken a chance? Truly letting go with no safety net to catch you if you fall? Having an undying faith in someone that means so much to you, that you forgot how you even existed before he or she came into your life?

Have you ever believed in something better? A better world perhaps? Where death is an honor to experience, and disease plays no part in it. A place where the worlds' evil cannot survive and love and trust is all we know.

That is a place that knows no pain, and that is where I want to go...

CHAPTER NINE

"When I wasn't happy I smiled anyway. I would stand in front of a mirror, and I would look at myself and practice smiling. Even though I did not like what I saw in that mirror then, I would do it regardless. Until eventually, my smiling became natural, and so did my happiness."

Every time I read this, it takes me back to a very difficult time of my life. Approximately lasting for almost two decades, I truly experienced, what it was to suffer. My internal strife was a gift that I did not ask for, nor desire. Today it is commonly known as "clinical depression." Granted, I am very aware that I was not happy as a small child, but it wasn't until I reached the age of fifteen years old, that this dark gift that I inherited, finally made its way into my bloodstream, my mind, and into my soul. The hold it had over me was crippling, but I refused to take medication. I decided that I would have to use my own mind to fight this battle and learn how to heal.

I recall clearly when it started. As I previously mentioned, it began when I was fifteen. I had fallen in love for the first time with a young woman, and it in the process I remember doing something to myself that I had never done before. You see, I had never been in love prior to her, and the feeling was extremely overwhelming. I was trying to process what I felt in my heart, while also trying to keep my mind from becoming overly saturated with love's euphoria. It was a difficult time for me. My prior experience of knowing love was very limited, and I had never really received it from the opposite sex, if that person didn't happen to be related to me. I guess I was doomed from the very beginning. The feeling I had mentioned, or the action that I decided to take against myself was now being put into play.

As each day that passed, and I fell more in love, I would lose a little more of myself. Although this woman did not hurt me or take advantage of my feelings for her, I began to abuse myself. I would do this by placing her up on a higher pedestal each day, and then loosening and lowering my own footing, until it got to a point, where I felt that I was no longer worthy of being with her. Why would anyone do that? Here I had someone that loved me dearly and wanted nothing, but the best for me. Yet I committed acts of self-hate and self inflicted damage. I realized then, that my childhood demons were coming closer to the surface.

I chose to purposely suffer, not realizing that it would last for many years afterwards, and would affect everyone that would come into contact with me. Damn those demons!

Shortly thereafter, I began to focus my attention on things that would fill the void I had within me. A permanent wound, that never seemed to stop bleeding out. I would have to find a way to help bandage it up. Perhaps a street gang would do the trick. I decided to bury myself in hatred. For it seemed that the only solution from heart-break, was to become a monstrous savage. Disconnecting from anything that could potentially hurt me seemed like the only logical decision. I had finally found my vice, and I celebrated and reveled in my new discovery.

Suddenly the pain was gone, but I wondered for how long? I decided not to focus on things that I did not have the answers to, and began to enjoy myself. It did not matter that I bathed in negativity, I was just happy to finally be able to feel complete. All the women in the world and their empty compliments or attempted insults, weren't enough to build me up or take me down. Now I was invincible. For the next twelve years, I would focus on being a violent and heartless creature. It seemed that the more I disconnected from my own humanity, the better it felt.

I lived day to day. For I never knew if I would survive another twenty-four hours. I would travel around my city purposely looking for perceived enemies to attack on site. No one that would play this "game" of gang banging, would win against my twin brother or myself. It was reckless and ruthless, and I deliberately put myself in harms way to show that I would always get the job done. The truth was, I was miserable. The void that I had filled wasn't always working as expected, and I just wanted someone to kill me. I wanted someone to take away the pain, to put me out of my misery.

Of course things never go according to plan, and I did have other needs in my life. By the time I was 25, something changed. I found myself tired of using women for my sadistic games. God must have been listening in. I fell madly in love with a woman, and it felt as if I was visiting heaven again. The war within me was raging for far too long, and I just needed some peace, but God wanted to give me just a little more. He decided to add to the celebration, and soon there after, I was to expect my first child. Alham'dulillah! (All praises due to God)

About two months after finding out this wonderful news, I decided to drop to my knees and pray. I wasn't a spiritual man or a religious man back then, so praying seemed foreign to me. Yet something told me to speak to God that day. As my knees touched the concrete outside of the local hospital that I just walked out of, I began to say these words, "Please, God please... I don't ask you for much, but today I humbly beg of you to do this one favor for me. My voice was beginning to tremble now. But I knew that dreams could only come true if you ask God to help you attain them."

My dream was my daughter, and that's exactly what I asked for…

Midway through the pregnancy, I realized that the relationship wasn't going to work. I decided to stay anyway. But our differences were to become overbearing, and I would be forced to leave before my daughter was even a year old. I was so hurt. I was so angry. I thought I had found the one I was going to spend the rest of my life with, but God had a different plan.

After mourning the death of the relationship with my daughter's mother, I realized I hadn't changed enough. For the hatred and anger I thought I had let go of, was still very much intact. I decided to revert back into a monster, and I dedicated the next three years to hurting every woman that was foolish enough to love me. Turmoil was all that I knew. Everything that I felt inside was now presenting itself in the outside world, and I didn't have the control I once had over it. It wasn't until my father passed away, that everything began to change.

It was then that I decided I didn't want to be a monster anymore. I didn't want to inflict my sickness onto others anymore either. One day I decided to look at myself in the mirror and tell myself that I was loved. I didn't believe it at first, but something inside of me was telling me not to stop, to give myself more credit, and to tell myself that I was worth it. I deserved happiness and I deserved peace. Finally my spirituality was born, and from that moment on, I never looked back.

CHAPTER TEN

"My father died with a picture of my mother in his hand, and that is definition of being loved by a man."

My father fell in love with my mother from the moment they first met. The story he told me, was that they were first were acquainted at a nightclub, through unexpected circumstances. He mentioned that because his feelings were so intense upon seeing her, that there was no possibility of him letting this woman pass him by. He claimed he was mesmerized by her beauty, and because of his confidence and a little bit of ego, he wouldn't allow himself to accept no for an answer from her.

You see my mother knew of my father's reputation long before they ever met, and one look at him, told her everything she needed to know about him, or so she thought. Let me just mention that my father was quite the ladies man. The attention that he would attract was something that had to be seen, to be believed. His energy was powerful, pure, somewhat angelic, but he also had a very dark side to him that many feared, and with good reason.

My mother played off my father at first, fearing of falling for someone who just wasn't right for her. She did desire a strong man though. A man's man, but she wouldn't give in so easily.

My father's persistence of my mother didn't exactly make it easy for her.

She soon would give in, and love would conquer both of their worlds. I would like to mention that my father chose at an early age to live what can be called "the street-life." He didn't attend college and certainly didn't have the funds to afford it either. He did however have a knack for doing whatever was needed to make ends meet, and perhaps even a little more.

My father was loved and respected wherever he found himself. I guess it was safe to say that he was sort of a gentle giant. The same name I would be given many years later.
If you were privileged enough to have known my father, then you would know that it was wise to never have mistaken his kindness for weakness. As loving and as affectionate as he was with my mother and his family, he could quickly revert into a ruthless savage if need be. No harm would ever come to his family as long as he was alive, he would often say. This was how he was known to myself and countless others. It may not seem like it was at all possible, from what little I have told you about him, but

the truth is, he was a gentleman, who was well mannered and very well spoken. He was adored wherever he went. For his energy was bigger than his body, and filled with much more good than bad.

His family life was what he lived for, and holidays in our home were celebrated in ways most would only dream of. My father loved us dearly. Although it never actually needed to be a holiday for him to want to always spoil his children. But I do recall Christmas mornings as a child, and what a time it was for us. My mother would always be in the kitchen preparing the feast, but would occasionally pop her head out of the kitchen to see the joy on the faces of her children that day. My father lived to make us smile, and he would make sure that every thing we wrote on our Christmas lists was given to us. You see, he had the need to over compensate for his children because of his lack of having his own father. So anything our little hearts desired, my father felt the need to acquire.
Now as I stated earlier, my father

was a true gentleman, and once I grew older, it was he who taught me how to properly love a woman. It was he who taught me about loyalty, honesty, and the small things that would make a positive impression on a woman. Always remembering to hold a door for her anywhere that I went, and certainly running towards the car door to open it for her, before she had an opportunity to open it for herself. These little things stuck with me, and I now will teach them to my daughter when it is time for her to take a man as her own.

My mother and father had a beautiful marriage. It was often admired by many of my childhood friends. For many of them, their parents were divorced. So when they saw the love between my mother and father, they would openly express their admiration for them. Problems did exist in their world, but the love they had for one another kept them together for twenty-five years. Eventually the honeymoon period would end, and my father's demons would wind up getting the best of him. It would cost him everything, including the love of his life.

After my parents divorced, I was forced to watch a man slowly deteriorate into someone I didn't even recognize. He became only a shadow of his former self, in which he would never recover from. I do recall doing whatever was necessary out of the love and respect for that man. With that being said, I do recall a particular occasion that still hurts me to this day. At this time my father was quite ill. He had lost all of his hair, and his beard was no longer groomed. I do remember it being all white, and I also remember the feel of it touching my face as I hugged and helped him up from his bed. He barely had any more strength in him, and some days he could barely recognize me.

For the pain of his inevitable death was growing closer, and today was the strongest reminder of what I was going to have to accept. He could barely say my name that day, and as he walked down the street to the store with me, he was hunched over and practically dragging his feet just to stay afloat. I did my best to remain strong and keep every tear inside my soul at bay. Once we finally reached the store, I approached the counter to ask the young lady for her assistance. But as soon as I had looked at her, she immediately saw all the cracks in my foundation. I was no longer able to hide my pain. Her eyes began to water and she asked me if I was ok. I looked back at her and I tried to speak, but the words just couldn't come out. I just stood there and began to cry. I don't remember leaving the store that day. Everything was a blur. I do recall asking God for his mercy on the soul of my father. Begging him to take him into paradise. I didn't want him to suffer any longer. He didn't deserve that.

It was not even a week after that, my father then passed away. The angel of death took my father to his final destination. I made a promise to my father the day he passed away, and although rigor mortis had already made its way into my father's shell, I still felt compelled to whisper these words into his ear, "I know your soul is no longer in this body, but I am aware that you could still hear me. I just want to say to you that I am proud to bear your last name, and honored to call myself your son. I will make you proud of me. I promise you."

Before stepping away from him, I began to notice something. It was a picture that he was holding in his hand. For you see, when it was finally time for my father to leave this world, he held onto the only thing that made him feel safe. The only person that could bring him comfort.

The love of his life, my mother…

CHAPTER ELEVEN

"Open Hands"

Do you really have any idea what I feel for you? Do you know what lives inside of me? Beneath the make believe surface, the hardened disconcerting looks, the armor-plated walls I have had up for almost as long as I have existed? Starting today, I want to do something different. I want to be honest with you. Honest in a way no man in history has ever been with a woman.

Honest in a way I've never been with anyone. Honest in a way that perhaps, could make me look weak... I am just tired of holding back. Tired of keeping me, to me...

Woman I can barely breathe while I write this...I am so in love with you...

I feel as if there aren't enough ways to show you what I feel, and I know at this exact moment, while I'm writing this to you, I'll never stop envisioning new ways to show you more. The truth is, I need this more than you know. For some reason when I think of us, I'm reminded of my childhood; all my failures. It seems that I never once finished anything that I've ever started...

So I need to finish this...

Between the battles I have had on the America's front lawn, and the warfare that still goes on at times inside of my head, you would assume that I would be better prepared for something like this. Possibly equipped with heavier artillery...

But it seems to me that all I've brought with me tonight are just these two things...

My heart on my sleeve,
        And
    "Open Hands."

CHAPTER TWELVE

**"I want to be everything you've
ever dreamt about. I want to be
everything every other man failed
to be. I want to help fill up the hole
that he left inside of you, and I
want to change the world with you
by my side. But most importantly,
I want to be the man that replaces
your father, when it's finally time
to give me your hand."**

Chivalry is not dead. And neither are
true gentlemen. We have to focus on
what is really important here. Before
we choose to complain to one
another about everyone else's
behavior, perhaps we should take a
look at our own. My idea of romance
and love comes from God, but the
respect for women came from my
father.

Think about that statement. Think of

the young men out there that don't have a father in their lives to teach them the difference between what is right and what is wrong. These young boys are left to learn from media outlets and friends who are in the same position as they are. The lack of respect for women is only the tip of the iceberg. Or what if the boys do have a father, or father figure in their lives, but are taught improperly? If the father is constantly cheating on his mother, and he admires his father obsessively, then the boy's chances of emulating his father's poor behavior, increases dramatically. I have actually seen this demonstrated amongst friends and strangers.

I was in Miami, Florida a few years ago, and I had the desire to see the water. The most logical decision was to make my way as quickly as possible to the beach. Upon walking for a few minutes near the shoreline, I began to notice something. It was a man and his son speaking loudly and acting like children. The father must have been in his forties, while his son was between the ages of 18-21.

It was sad what I saw that day. A young girl around the age of seventeen began to walk by. Upon passing the two men, the father told his son, "Look at her ass – I love your mother, but she isn't enough to satisfy my cravings. I would give it to that little girl." The son laughed and began to say inappropriate things about her as well. I couldn't believe what I was witnessing. That little girl didn't deserve those vulgar comments, but I also found myself concerned with something else, something just as important to me. I thought to myself,
"Who taught these two men how to behave?"

A better way to phrase it would be, where did it start and when? The young man obviously learned this from his father or lack there of, but who taught the older man? This broken behavior may have been carried on long before these two were created, and that concerned me. Imagine the amount of broken women that bloodline alone may have ruined.

This is the way that I find myself thinking many a times. I realize that there has to be a way to break the cycle for others, the same way I was able to break away from my own ignorance. Patience is something that can take a lifetime to master, or more than one. But I pray daily and ask for more of it from God, especially when it comes to sensitive subjects such as this one. I'm also a father to a little girl. So what's to become of her, or what kind of men will she meet once she becomes of age? It is my responsibility to be the man that leads by example, and be the proof to her, that good men exist. I am nowhere near perfect, but I definitely try my hardest to be, and make sure to always lead with my heart, as opposed to my ego. There are good men out there, loyal men as well, I happen to know some, which does give me hope.

I think of the kind of man that I am. I then think about the kind of woman I see myself marrying. She would need to be Spiritual like myself. Her race is of no importance, but her belief and love of God will determine everything. You have to remember that commonalities are what keep you together and in agreement. Your differences are simply what make you unique, but to have a true connection and powerful love for God as a union, is something worth cherishing. We will have a love that will change both of our lives, and the lives of anyone whom we come across. A strong energy and union, that shows unification and true admiration for each other.

Once these key points are established, I feel it would be necessary to marry her. But there are steps and an understanding that would need to take place before any of this can become a reality.

This is where the knowledge that my father passed onto me would be put into play. If this woman is blessed enough to have her father around, and he also plays an active role within her life, then it now becomes my responsibility to sit with this man, and to speak to him about my intention when it comes to his daughter. Granted, I most likely

would have met him prior to this
encounter, so our relationship would
be a good one, but with this serious
topic at hand, a private sit down is
necessary. It shows respect and
humbleness. Traits that God himself
approves of.

If he agrees, that I am the man for his
daughter, then it's smooth sailing
from there, but if he does not, then I
would try my hardest to convince
him that his decision is wrong, and
would kindly pursue him until he
changes his mind. After receiving his
approval, not much would change.
For the fact remains that I would
have already been treating his
daughter as a queen, prior to our
meeting. The only things that would
change, are the fact that his daughter
will now share my last name, and
that we will be living together as a
family unit.

The proposal is obviously something
I wouldn't reveal in this book
(laughs) but it would be the done
properly nevertheless. For a true
queen deserves a king of strength,
but also of extreme respect and

humbleness. Just listen to your heart, because that's God speaking to you.

CHAPTER THIRTEEN

"Why do so many men run towards a war, but run away from love? Perhaps the more important battle you need to face is not in another country, but in fact, inside of you."

How long have men run away from the only entity that can bring them closer to God? I know far too many men that leave relationships that can actually help them flourish. Either that, or they self sabotage every relationship they are in, right up until the day that they die. A sad reality. A sad truth.

I remember being around nineteen years old and attending a university in New York City. There was a young man in my classroom, who stood out to me. He was very open about his life and about his issues, and would discuss them with anyone that was willing to listen. The day soon came where we would all be forced to listen to this young man's testimony.

The professor asked him to speak in front of the class that particular day, and what he shared was nothing short of heart breaking. He began to speak of his sexual conquests, and the problem he had within those conquests. Claiming that he always really liked every woman that he met, until the day would eventually come where he would sleep with them. After the act was completed, all interest in knowing more about them was lost. The connection was then broken, and off he went to find his next victim, to make the same mistake again. It was sad to see such a young man so unhappy. I wonder how his life was prior to meeting him in that classroom. Who raised him and what was lacking in his household? Did he have a father to teach him right from wrong? Was his father the one that taught him this broken way of thinking? Or did he have a father at all? I realized that this man was far from God. I was aware that I was as well, but this young man's words really disturbed me. This man knew nothing of a genuine connection, and that scared me.

I often think about all the men that I know that cheat on their wives. I know of one in particular that claims that he can't help himself, because of the overwhelming feeling that he settled in his marriage. For the fact remains that he doesn't find his wife very attractive, but would never leave due to certain financial obligations and the fact that they have children. Despite all the alcohol that this man consumes, and all the women that he sleeps with, none of it can bring his soul the joy he craves for. Years later, I am sad to report that his behavior hasn't changed much. What I find most disturbing is the fact that his wife knows of his indiscretions, and still decides to stay. This woman knows nothing of her worth. For if she did know, she would have walked away some time ago. Perhaps if he would finally open his eyes, he would realize that his wife is an angel.

We need to understand that his decisions and others that partake in similar behavior aren't all just selfish. There is something else that exists in more men than women (in my opinion) and seems to strike fear in a way that even death does not. It is the fear of vulnerability.

As a man, and speaking from experience, I can look back at the mistakes I have made throughout my life, and recognize those same mistakes in others. I believe it was necessary to make those mistakes and suffer through them as well, so that I could help the people of today, especially our men. I also realize that today's daughters are tomorrow's mothers, and I can't bear to see another generation of women being broken at the hands of more broken men. We need to teach our sons that vulnerability is a part of love and a part of life. It's also the only way to find God. There is definitely a trust issue at hand, and we need to figure out a way past it. I am not spilling the beans here on why men do what they do; I'm simply being honest. I believe these issues always begin during our childhood. If our fathers and mothers learned how to communicate properly with one another, then they would also communicate better with their children. When we are conditioned to respond to falling in love with fear, as opposed to embracing it whole-heartedly as a celebration, the repercussions become catastrophic. Generations of men and women are doomed and become victims of a broken repeated behavior. When do we break the cycle, and how?

What we need are more people to come forth and spread the word of love. In this case I would say it should be the men. I often find myself speaking to the youth and explaining to them that what they see glorified on television isn't the way to happiness, but rather the easiest way to become sad, broken, empty, and lonely. We have to teach our sons the true value of women, and that only through them; we can reach a higher or satisfying "state of being."

I also for one grew tired of saying goodbye to the one's I loved, and no longer wish to see any more tears fill the eyes of our female companions. I was once told by a woman that I would end up like my father; broken and alone, until death would find me. While those words were harsh, & should have never been said, I still appreciated them. For they reminded me of what can become of any of us, if we don't choose love. If we don't choose God.

CHAPTER FOURTEEN

"I want to build something that will be here when I no longer am."

Let's start with kindness. An important trait that I feel everyone should possess. I realize that if more people were just kinder to one another, humanity wouldn't have the problems that it faces today. I truthfully do not see the difficulty in being kind to anyone. Please take notice to the fact that I mentioned the word kind, as opposed to using the word nice. For those that may not know, there is a significant difference. Kindness comes from within. It shows true character and more importantly, proves that humanity has hope. You are kind to those that do not directly benefit you. You are kind to them because you realize that we are all connected, and showing others kindness, is a reflection of who you are. Being nice says a lot about you as well. It says to the world, that it's more a chore for you than anything. These are the kind of people who lack a genuine nature to them. I prefer to steer clear of them. For you never know when they will reveal their other face. Which brings me back to the title of this chapter, and to that first paragraph.

As I have mentioned before, I used to be one of those people. Cold, calculated, and disconnected. I was unkind. But after having life throw me back a few curve balls, I found my way back to a place that seemed familiar. I genuinely care about humanity, and I am trying to do something to change the world, & I do this by opening up my heart and life to everyone. For some, my words may seem too personal, but this is how God made me. So this is how I choose to express and deliver his message.

I am always discussing the topic of love and with good reason. For there is never a time to not spread it. I believe that there should be more mosques built. There should be more synagogues and churches built as well. If your religion preaches love, then why not create a place where the worship of love is celebrated?

We should also spend more time outside with nature. Looking at all the animals, all the trees, the flowing water, and the smell of the air. For even that air is a gift from God, and that makes it important enough to be celebrated!

You may be wondering what I plan on building myself, or leaving behind, but I think as you read these words, you should already have the answer. I'm planting ideas in the minds of every reader and with every word that I speak or write. These ideas may consist of the following. The idea of happiness, the idea of peace, the idea of kindness, and the idea that love can save humanity. That it can save us from ourselves.

I have an undying belief in what I say and what I feel. The messages that I share with all of you, comes from somewhere deep within my soul. A place only God and myself can visit. These ideas that I speak of are real, and they are what truly matters. For they also have a real frequency. It all comes to down to understanding, kindness, & love. Things that many of us have been lacking, or haven't been shown for far too long. It only takes one act of kindness to change someone's life. From there it can then spread, and turn into a positive wildfire for everyone to feel its warmth.

I work out consistently, and where I get my motivation from, isn't from where many would assume. Granted there are many great athletes to admire, and that I am friends with, but it is those that are just beginning to find their way, that give me the most inspiration and joy. A few weeks ago I met a woman in the gym. The first thing I noticed about her was her energy. She was a very good person. The next thing I noticed was her weight. For it was hard not to notice that this woman was obese. I smiled at her, because I saw her there making the effort to save her own life.

For the next several weeks I kept seeing her. Eventually I began to waving to her and saying hello. I was very proud of her, and each every time that I saw her, I made sure to tell her exactly that. People just need positive reassurance sometimes. How am I to know if anyone had ever been kind to her? What if everyone always made fun of her because of her weight, or didn't like her for any other ridiculous reason? I always remember what it felt like to not like myself, and how much it hurt when others inflicted their hurtful words on me. It's easy to believe the ugly words that others say to you, when you're told them every day. This is especially true, when it begins during your childhood. The truth is, I not only admired this woman's courage to do something about her health, but I genuinely cared about her as well.

I recall having to go to the pharmacy one day, perhaps to grab a favorite candy bar of mine, and a few other things. While roaming through the aisles, I noticed a little boy who was quite rambunctious. I also noticed that he was autistic. As soon as he noticed me, he immediately ran up to me. He brought up the fact that he loved my beard and asked if he could touch it. With a smile on my face I replied "absolutely." After admiring the texture of my facial hair, he quickly said to me. "Wow you have impressive guns!" He then asked me, "Can I show you mine? I replied with an astounding yes, and he then made the best body builder pose he could think of. I smiled and told him. "You're in better shape then I am!" He laughed, hugged me, and then went his way. I stood there frozen. Paralyzed in fact. The feeling for me was just too overwhelming. This boy, this stranger, had such an effect on me. He had not a care in the world, and had more love inside of him, than I've seen in this whole world. I was completely convinced that this boy was a gift from our creator. He humbled me, and at that moment I felt closer to God.

You see the point of life is to find the deepest of loves, and then to spread that same love to those that are lacking it in their lives. It's also proof that you don't need money to leave something behind for others to follow or emulate. Our world's top spiritual scholars all agree, that love and God are of the same entity. Whether you accept that or not, it doesn't make it any less true. If you truly want to leave something beautiful behind when your human form is no longer here, simply spread love to your friends and family. Especially to your children. That love will exist and live in their hearts, long after we are gone; and what better gift to leave behind than the gift of love?

The gift of God...

CHAPTER FIFTEEN

"There are two reasons why we suffer. The first is to teach us a lesson. The second, is so that our children won't have to…"

Suffering is necessary for emotional and spiritual development. Sadly, this is the only way many of us can learn what happiness is. I also believe this was the case long before I ever existed. Long before any of us ever existed. I believe that life is a test, and that our existence on this earth boils down to nothing but this test. The thing is, this same test can be as simple or complicated as you choose to make it.

The film "The Matrix" makes a lot more sense to me these days. While everyone is busy being distracted by the great story telling and action within the film, they are all forgetting the important story hidden beneath the sci-fi shell. Trust me, I am definitely a fan of the film myself, but this is about searching for depth. Somehow the world has gotten lost in the nonsense of surface deep entertainment, and has forgotten what living is all about. It's not being about a straight arrow either. For anyone that walks the path, without ever raising their head to look at what is around them, will eventually walk off a cliff.

Life is about being good and giving back. That much I do know. I also recognize that the journey has many layers to it, and it's easy to get lost in any of one them. That is why so many people stay at the same frequency, or in the same position, which then leads them to make the same mistakes for their entire lives. Think about how many people you have outgrown. How many people were you forced to leave behind, that you cared about or possibly loved? These are the people that get lost in the mazes of their own lives. What they don't realize is that these problems are all self created. Some go mad and lose themselves, while others just give up and settle for whatever comes into their lives. Especially when it comes to relationships. I know far too many people that have fallen into the settlement arena, and watching it is emotionally exhausting. It's no wonder that they have become like zombies, and walk with their heads down whenever you see them. I always make sure to pray for them, because their self esteem and spirits are now broken.

I must admit, I've repeated a lesson or two more than once myself. I was quite a stubborn boy, and my mind and soul paid the cost. From my dysfunctional relationships with women, to the violent acts as a once active gang member, everything was all part of my test. I chose the harder route willingly, and I have no regrets.

Though when I look back, it wasn't easy getting through the things I was forced to. It was either that, or let the guilt of my shameful actions and behavior break me down and ruin

any chance of finding my sanity &
happiness. I played a game of
Russian roulette with my own mind,
and I recall crying myself to sleep
more times than I would care to
admit right now. The thoughts of my
victims and the horrific things I had
done, would play over in my mind
like a bad dream. Yet I was never
asleep, and I knew that one day, I
would have to face my karma. Don't
you see? I too was caught up in a
deep cycle of darkness, which I
repeated continuously for years.
Seeing my friends die and going to
jail, still didn't break me away from
the vicious cycle of gang banging. I
was attracted to negativity, and it
would be many years before I would
ever find myself, or God.

Today I heard a story that seems far
too common these days. A friend
reached out to me from overseas, and
was crying to me over the phone.
What she immediately began to tell
me was heart wrenching. For you
see, her sister had come over to her
mother's flat, and had a blackened
eye again. This was a gift given
courtesy of her husband. I am not

sure what I found more disturbing. The fact that her husband beats on her almost daily, or the fact that this young woman always find herself running back to him. I was told that this has been happening for over twelve years now, and each and every time it would happen, she would tell everyone that she is simply clumsy, and has accidents frequently.

No one ever believed her stories, but no one ever said anything to her either, except for my friend. Today she finally spoke up for her sister, and that would make her nothing less than a hero. I am not certain what's going to happen, from this day forth in regards to that unhealthy marriage, but I do hope that this young lady realizes that this is not what God would want for her. I do have a message to her that I would like her to hear. So I hope that somehow, this book makes it into your hands, so that you see that someone from across the world, who may never meet you, still cares about you. Young lady, sister, & mother. You are in fact a gift from God. I heard that your physical beauty had gotten you many proposals in the past, but I have also heard that your soul is more beautiful than your shell, & for that reason alone, I want to remind you that you are loved.

There will be those that will be surprised that I offer my heart this way to strangers, but that fact that anyone would be surprised is what is actually quite sad. People are so concerned with their own lives and possible problems, that they will purposely ignore someone who may be crying in the home that is just next door to them. I can't live my life that way. Granted, I am not a nosey or intrusive person, but if I happen to see someone who may need my help, I will help them as often as I can. Just the other day I went and gave a few dollars to a homeless man. The person that I was with at the time remarked, "He's just going to use it on drugs or alcohol" I replied, "That isn't my concern. God knows my intention and my heart, and that man needed my help."

Which brings me to an important subject, the topic of my daughter. It seems that any time I have ever gone through emotional turmoil, I've actually learned something. Sometimes about myself, and other times about life. So while the pain may resonate for a while, the lesson resonates for the rest of my life. I also purposely chose to suffer in my past, and believe that I had chosen to do so, before I was created in this body. I'm no messiah, and I am no prophet either. I just feel things inside of me that tell me that this true. For I didn't pass on my demons to my daughter, the way that they were passed on to me, & that is my proof. I believe I suffered in this life for her, so that she would not have to. I know that she will face some of her own pain as she grows older, but that will be minimal compared to what I chose to endure for her. She is everything that I would want a human being to be and more. She is better than me, and that is all I ever wanted for her. I remind her every day of who she is. My heart, a part of my soul, a princess who will one day

be a queen, and most importantly,
my saving grace.

I want to say thank you to everyone
who decided to purchase my book. I
truly hope it touches your lives, just
as much as it touched mine to write
it. I once had a person say to me,
"Mr. North, so much of your writing
makes me cry every time that I read
it."
I replied,
"It should, because I was crying
when I wrote it."
These days I am happier than I have
ever been in my life, but I still
needed to share my ups and downs to
prove that all of us are in this
together. I love all of you and thank
you for taking the time to get to
know me a little bit more about me.
For these words are a testimony
bearing my truth.
For this is the

naked soul, of a bearded man…

AUTHOR'S NOTE

I began writing when I was a child. It was a way for me to express myself freely, and it provided me with a feeling of safety and empowerment, that I felt nowhere else but there, in that moment, through unedited literature. I won't sit here and tell the world that I had the worst childhood, because that certainly wasn't the case. But when those moments of loneliness and sadness made their way into my world, the only friends I recall having by my side were a pen and paper. It wasn't until later, that I learned that my writing wasn't just fueled through heartache and loss, but through life's happiest and touching moments as well. After writing numerous pieces for the

world to see, I felt it was only fair
that I shared more of me.

I write for my niece. For she needs to
know how much I truly love her, and
this here is my proof. A public
document for the entire world to see,
especially you! I write in hopes that
somehow it will grant me the ability
to give you a better home to live in.
 For your eyes are filled with pain
and sorrow that haunt me more often
than I care to admit. The world's hate
is right outside of your front door,
and I can no longer stand here,
pretending that it does not affect you,
myself, and of course my brother,
your father. Such innocence
shouldn't know such pain. From my
heart to yours, from my lips to God's
ears, I will rescue you. I promise.

I write for the sick. Let me be your
beacon of hope. Someone to help
ease your pain. If you happen to lose
all faith in God, then please, share
your troubles and struggles with me.
For I am simply a caring stranger
who is here to listen. At some point
when the pain becomes too much to
bear, you may feel free to place it

upon my chest. I will then gladly
wear that burden and dress it as my
own until it subsides. I've held the
weight of the world on my shoulders
for longer than I could possibly
remember, so what is a few more
pounds to wear? I do not need to
know you personally, to share my
empathy and my love with you. I
know it's hard to believe, but there
are some of us that remain good in
this world. Let my existence be proof
of that.

I write for my mother. I write with
hopes that you will someday smile
again from the inside out, and that
my writing will remind you of how
much your existence matters to
everyone, especially me. I write in
hopes that the love you still carry for
my father, will somehow grant you
the ability to meet him again after
this life, and that you two will spend
eternity together where it matters
most.

I write because I believe in others.
Call me a fool; call me naive, doubt
every ounce of me, and it still won't

change my undying belief in humanity.

I write for anyone who won't find their inner talent, until they are inside of a box. Too many of my friends know exactly what I mean by that. Let my writing change the course of your life.

I write for anyone who has ever felt alone. Let my writing prove that you're wrong, and that you have a friend that you simply haven't met yet.

I write for those who feel different. Learn that difference is an attribute that far too many of us do not embrace. Ask yourself if you really want to be just like everyone else? Or would you prefer to be remembered for standing out? I know that I do.

I write for anyone who has ever lost someone dear to them. Understand that there are no mistakes, and that the souls of your loved one's were carried on the wings of angels to their proper destination. May you find solace in these words.

I write because I want to stand for something bigger than myself. Change perhaps? If I can help a single person recognize their wrong doing, and change their self for the better, than I have accomplished exactly what I was meant to do while I am here.

I write for my daughter. Let me be the best father to you. Let my writing show you exactly who I am, and let these words be an example of how you deserve to be loved by a man.

I write because I'm afraid. Afraid of failure? Or am I afraid of success? Perhaps I'm just afraid that I have nothing else to offer the world. Nothing but this, nothing but my writing…

31896038R00062

Made in the USA
San Bernardino, CA
08 April 2019